Essential Events

THE OREGON TRAIL

BY MARCIA AMIDON LUSTED

Content Consultant

Eric Morser, assistant professor of American history
Skidmore College

ABDO
Publishing Company

CREDITS

Published by ABDO Publishing Company, 8000 West 78th Street, Edina, Minnesota 55439. Copyright © 2012 by Abdo Consulting Group, Inc. International copyrights reserved in all countries. No part of this book may be reproduced in any form without written permission from the publisher. The Essential Library™ is a trademark and logo of ABDO Publishing Company.

Printed in the United States of America, North Mankato, Minnesota
062011
092011

Editor: Paula Lewis
Copy Editor: Rebecca Rowell
Interior Design and Production: Kazuko Collins
Cover Design: Kazuko Collins

Library of Congress Cataloging-in-Publication Data
Lusted, Marcia Amidon.
   The Oregon Trail / by Marcia Amidon Lusted.
      p. cm. -- (Essential events)
   Includes bibliographical references.
   ISBN 978-1-61783-102-7
   1. Oregon National Historic Trail--Juvenile literature. 2. Frontier and pioneer life--West (U.S.)--Juvenile literature. 3. Overland journeys to the Pacific--Juvenile literature. 4. West (U.S.)--History--19th century--Juvenile literature. 5. Oregon Territory--History--Juvenile literature. I. Title.
   F597.L97 2012
   978'.02--dc22
                                        2011007942

TABLE OF CONTENTS

Emigrants moved in wagon trains to the West.

THE LONG TRAIL WEST

In the spring of 1844, nine-year-old Catherine Sager headed for Oregon in a wagon train. With her parents and six siblings, the family was one of a group of emigrants traveling together for safety. Her father, Henry Sager, was a restless man who kept moving his family farther west to find better and less expensive land for farming.

Years later, Catherine remembered leaving Missouri to take the Oregon Trail west, knowing that it was unlikely she would ever see extended family members and friends again:

> *Many friends came that far to see the emigrants start on their long journey, and there was much sadness at the parting, and a sorrowful company crossed the Missouri that bright spring morning. The motion of the wagon made us all sick, and it was weeks before we got used to the seasick motion. Rain came down and required us to tie down the wagon covers, and so increased our sickness by confining the air we breathed.*[1]

Catherine's story was more dramatic than most. She survived a massacre when Native Americans killed her adopted parents. Yet, her experiences reflect those of nearly 500,000 pioneers who traveled on a path called the Oregon Trail between 1840 and the Civil War (1861–1865). People uprooted their families from their homes, farms, and businesses

"There is enchantment in the word [Oregon]. It signifies a laden of pure delight in the woody solitudes of the West. . . . That is a country of the largest liberty, the only known land of equality on the face of the earth . . . there is a place to build anew the Temple of Democracy."[2]

—*Cleveland* Plain Dealer *newspaper, 1843*

to travel to a place they had never even seen. What little they knew came from guidebooks, which often provided an optimistic and incorrect view of the journey.

SEEKING A BETTER LIFE

Those who traveled the Oregon Trail wanted a better life for their families. Farmers in places such as New England struggled with rocky soil and short growing seasons. The stories of rich, black soil in the Great Plains and the Pacific coast were enticing. A Missouri farmer explained why he wanted to go to Oregon:

> Out in Oregon I can get me a square mile of land. . . . I am done with the country [here]. Winters it's frost and snow to freeze a body; summers the overflow from [the Mississippi River] drowns half my acres; taxes take the yield of them that's left.[3]

An economic depression and waves of epidemic illnesses also drove people to seek new places to live. These factors, as well as simple curiosity, restlessness, and a desire for adventure, motivated thousands of individuals and families to seek a new life. Many traveled 2,000 miles (3,219 km) by wagon, often walking most of the way, covering only 15–20 miles (24.1–32.1 km) on a good day. These pioneers called themselves emigrants because they were leaving the United States and heading into unknown territory.

Often starting in Independence, Missouri, the emigrants traveled west to cross the Rocky Mountains at South Pass. At this point, the trail forked. A decision had to be made whether to travel northwest toward Oregon or southwest toward California. They gambled on the weather, knowing they had to leave Missouri by April 15 in order to reach Oregon

A Difficult Decision

Crowded conditions and a lack of sewage and sanitary systems contributed to increasingly unhealthiness in the eastern cities of the United States. This was a major factor in the decision to emigrate westward. For many years, the number of deaths from yellow fever outnumbered births in New Orleans, Louisiana, and other areas along the Mississippi River. Epidemics of cholera raged for decades, killing tens of thousands of people.

Many merchants, doctors, ministers, teachers, and farmers were lured to the West. It held the promise of free land and a new beginning. Still, making the decision to travel westward on the Oregon Trail was not taken lightly. It was a difficult trip to endure and one filled with uncertainty and hardships.

An estimated 10 percent of all the emigrants who traveled the trail died on the way, accounting for more than 20,000 deaths. Illnesses were the leading killer. Due to the inexperience of the emigrants, accidents with firearms and wagons added to the death toll. Some emigrants drowned when crossing rivers. Murder, deaths during fights, and attacks by Native Americans received a great deal of attention in the press, but these were actually a minor percentage of all deaths on the trail.

before winter. At times, wagons were hauled up steep mountainsides with ropes and pulleys. At other times, wagons were floated across dangerous river crossings. A wrong turn, an illness, or the loss of oxen or a wagon could result in a delay and spending the winter in the wilderness with insufficient supplies.

Despite the hardships of the trail, most of those who set out from the civilized East were enthusiastic and hopeful. Among the hardships, they also experienced anticipation and good times. Nancy Hembree Snow Bogart, who traveled west with her family in 1843, wrote of her journey:

> *I've often been asked if we did not suffer with fear in those days but I've said no we did not have sense enough to realize our danger . . . since I've grown older and could realize the danger and the feelings of the mothers, I often wonder how they really lived through it all and retained their reason.* [4]

At the End of the Trail

The emigrants who were lucky reached British Fort Vancouver, which was the first military post constructed to protect and outfit the newly arriving settlers. Doctor John McLoughlin was in charge of

Fort Vancouver provided emigrants a place to rest before continuing on the last part of their journey.

the self-sufficient fort. Under his supervision, the fort supported his men as well as the travelers who were nearing their final stop—Oregon City was across the river. In addition to growing fruit, vegetables, and grain, the fort had a general store, a church, a school, a theater, and a library. Once the pioneers were rested, they crossed the river and began looking for land to construct homes, start farms, and begin their new lives.

In 1853, approximately ten years after Catherine Sager's family migrated west, Amelia Stewart Knight traveled to Oregon from Iowa. Keeping a diary of the trip from April to September, she wrote of finally reaching Oregon:

> *It has cleared off and we are all ready for a start again, for some place we don't know where. . . . We picked up and ferried across the Columbia River, utilizing skiff, canoes and flatboat to get across, taking three days to complete. Here husband traded two yoke of oxen for a half section of land with one-half acre planted to potatoes and a small log cabin and lean-to with no windows. This is the journey's end.[5]*

Almost 500,000 emigrants set out along the Oregon Trail between 1840 and 1860. They carried with them the hopes and dreams for a better life. Some would arrive in what many called the Promised Land. But others would lose everything—even their lives. ⌒

Eleven Children

Narcissa Whitman was one of the first white women to cross the Rocky Mountains. She and her husband established the Whitman mission. They took in many children—including the Sager children—whose parents died on the Oregon Trail. In a letter home, she wrote, "You will be astonished to know that we [now] have eleven children in our family, and not one of them our own by birth, but so it is. Seven orphans were brought to our door in October 1844, whose parents both died on the way to this country. Destitute and friendless, there was no other alternative—we must take them in or they must perish."[6]

A marker along the Oregon Trail

Thomas Jefferson was president when the United States made the Louisiana Purchase.

An Expanding Country

As settlers and immigrants arrived in what would become the United States, they continually pushed westward across the continent, seeking more land and new places to live in territories such as Kentucky and Ohio.

The West was considered to be the area between the Appalachian Mountains and the Mississippi River.

However, until the early years of the nineteenth century, much of the continent belonged to other countries, including Spain and France. Until 1801, Spain controlled the Louisiana Territory, which included the port of New Orleans. In a secret treaty between Spain and France, Eastern and Western Florida and Louisiana, which included New Orleans, became French territory.

In 1801, President Thomas Jefferson realized the need to expand the United States for shipping and access to the Gulf coast. He also understood the importance and possible consequences of the Napoleonic Wars throughout the European countries that owned large chunks of North America's western territory. Jefferson considered how the US government could guarantee Americans who settled in the western territories that they would not be affected by foreign events.

THE LOUISIANA PURCHASE

Jefferson instructed Robert R. Livingston, his minister to France, to extend an offer on behalf of the United States to France to buy New Orleans.

The port city was important for US trade and the adjoining territory. In 1803, Napoléon Bonaparte agreed to sell New Orleans and all of the Louisiana Territory, a total of 828,000 square miles (2,144,520 sq km), to the United States for $15 million. Instead of purchasing just a city, the United States had bought half a continent at the bargain price of approximately four cents per acre (0.4 ha).

General Horatio Gates summed up the transaction when he said to Jefferson, "Let the land rejoice, for you have bought Louisiana for a song."[1] The Louisiana Purchase, as it came to be called, doubled the size of the United States almost overnight. Settlers now had access to the Mississippi River trade route as well as a new area of settlement between the known United States and the Rocky Mountains. The area contained natural resources that were richer than anyone could have imagined.

In Search of a Northwest Passage

Jefferson was eager to learn more about this new territory. Once any American explorers left US territory, however, they would be traveling on foreign soil. England owned the northern strip of territory beyond the western boundary of the

Louisiana Purchase. Spain owned the southern part. Any expedition traveling westward across the entire continent included traveling across at least one of these foreign territories, meaning any government-sponsored expedition needed to be done in secret. A westward expedition would also encounter many different tribes of native peoples. Their rights over the land were not fully recognized by the United States and nations such as France, Spain, and England.

Jefferson understood the importance of exploring the new territory and

Unconstitutional?

President Thomas Jefferson believed in a strict interpretation of the US Constitution. As a result, he had doubts about whether the federal government really had the authority to purchase foreign territory such as the Louisiana Purchase. The Constitution did not expressly state that this type of purchase was acceptable. Opponents of the purchase based their protests on that omission.

Many thought the United States already had too much land and not enough money to spend on acquiring more. Harrison Gray Otis, a former congressman of Massachusetts, said, "I would rather the Mississippi River were a running stream of burning lava, over which no human being could pass, than that the [Louisiana Purchase] treaty be ratified."[2]

But Jefferson knew if he waited for a constitutional amendment to be created and passed, he might lose the opportunity to gain the land for the United States and risk war with France. Jefferson admitted to stretching his authority and made the decision to go ahead with the purchase. He stated, "What is practicable must often control what is pure theory."[3] Most Americans were excited about his decision.

*An early map of the Louisiana Purchase in 1803;
the boundaries were modified later by treaty.*

gathering information about the animals and plants
of the region, many of which no Euro-American had
ever seen. He also had another motive for organizing
an exploratory expedition. Jefferson wanted to find
a northwest passage—a direct water route to link
the United States with the Pacific coast. This would
provide the most direct and practical transportation
for merchants and emigrants to travel west since
water travel was simpler and easier than going by
wagon or on horseback.

With this in mind, and before the Louisiana
Purchase had been formalized, Jefferson approached

the US Congress in January 1803. He asked for funding for an expedition to find a water route to the Pacific Ocean and collect scientific data. The British were already involved in fur trading with the Native Americans in the Northwest. Jefferson hoped a US expedition would also establish trade with these tribes. He estimated that the cost of an expedition would be minimal. Congress approved $2,500 for the expedition.

Jefferson now had to choose the leaders of this important expedition. He approached his private secretary, 28-year-old Captain Meriwether Lewis, who had experience with the frontier and Native Americans. Lewis, in turn, chose a coleader, William Clark, who also had frontier experience. Together, they selected the men who would accompany them and make up the Corps of Discovery.

On May 14, 1804, after months of planning and with more than 40 men in the expedition, Clark and most of the men departed from Camp DuBois aboard the keelboat *Discovery*.

The Louisiana Territory

In 1804, the US Congress named the Louisiana Purchase lands the Territory of Orleans. In 1812, the Territory of Orleans was admitted to the United States as the state of Louisiana. The remaining land from the Louisiana Purchase eventually became all or part of Arkansas, Colorado, Iowa, Kansas, Minnesota, Missouri, Montana, Nebraska, New Mexico, North Dakota, Oklahoma, South Dakota, Texas, and Wyoming.

A few of the men paddled alongside the *Discovery* in two pirogues. The expedition traveled westward on the Missouri River and met up with Lewis six days later in Saint Charles, Missouri.

With the Louisiana Purchase, much of the territory that the expedition covered was now part of the United States. The expedition traveled north and west across the entire continent. One of the most famous members of Lewis and Clark's expedition was a Native American woman named Sacajawea. She was the wife of a French-Canadian trapper, Toussaint Charbonneau, who was hired as a guide and interpreter for the expedition. Many historians consider that she played a major role in the success of the trip. Her knowledge of Native American sign language enabled her to communicate with many of the tribes they encountered.

Eighteen months later, in November 1805, the expedition reached the Pacific coast. Clark wrote in his journal:

> We are in view of the Ocean, this great Pacific Ocean which we [have] been so long anxious to see, and the roaring or noise made by the waves breaking on the rocky shores . . . may be heard distinctly.[4]

On a high point overlooking the ocean, Clark later carved a message into the bark of a tree: "William Clark, December 3rd, 1805. By Land. From the U. States."[5]

Lewis and Clark believed they had found a practical passage for traveling across the entire continent of North America. In reality, the route they took was too difficult for wagons to travel. Though they failed to establish an easy way for emigrants to reach Oregon, the explorers discovered much about the previously unknown West. It was no longer a mystery. They had taken the first steps that would ultimately lead to the Great Migration along the Oregon Trail.

But before the migration began, other Americans blazed trails into the West. In August 1805, Lieutenant Zebulon Pike of the US Army had led a group of 20 soldiers north from Saint Louis, Missouri. Their goal was to explore the upper part of the

The Great Plains Barrier

The Louisiana Purchase opened up vast new areas of the country for settlement. However, settlers viewed the Great Plains and the mountain regions as barriers to be crossed in reaching the desirable lands in California and Oregon. The plains region was considered undesirable because it lacked timber for building, rivers for transporting goods to markets, and sufficient rainfall. It was not until the second part of the nineteenth century and the acquisition of land from Native American tribes that emigrants began to realize the agricultural potential of the Great Plains.

Mississippi River to find its source and purchase land from the Dakota.

In April 1806, Pike returned to Saint Louis. His expedition was considered a failure. He had not found the source of the Mississippi River or discovered any lakes or rivers that had not already been mapped.

Pike later explored the Southwest and New Mexico. These expeditions added to the knowledge of the new territories. Some were successful; others resulted in failure and even death—but all ultimately enticed restless Americans to go west.

A bronze statue of Meriwether Lewis, William Clark, and Sacagawea

Chapter 3

Fur traders with pelts on the Bear River in Utah

THE TRAILBLAZERS

Beaver and otter pelts were fashionable in North America and Europe for making waterproof hats and coats. As the demand for these furs increased, the supply of these animals in the eastern United States diminished. Trappers needed a new source of furs. When they heard reports from the Lewis and Clark expedition that there was a plentiful supply of these animals in the Pacific Northwest, British and Americans took advantage of this new territory.

FURS

Many of the men who set out for these lucrative new trapping grounds established exclusive rights to trade with Native American tribes such as the Osage. Manuel Lisa operated his fur trade by making a deal with the Native Americans along the Osage River in what is now Kansas. The tribes trapped beaver and otter and sold them only to Lisa. In 1807, Lisa expanded his trade by taking a party of men across what is now Montana along the Yellowstone River. There, the men constructed the Fort Raymond trading post. This fort was the first non-Native American settlement in that area.

In 1809, Lisa became one of the founders of the St. Louis Missouri Fur Company for another expedition. This group's responsibility was to continue the trading relationship with the Crow tribe. However, working with Native Americans to harvest and trade furs was not always successful. In

Fur trader John Jacob Astor

1810, a fur trading party was raided several times by Blackfeet war parties, and five trappers were killed. This discouraged many fur traders from making expeditions in the West.

One of the men involved in the fur trade was John Jacob Astor of New York. In addition to looking for new sources of fur, he was also interested in finding a quick way to Oregon to use the Pacific coast as a shorter sailing route to China. A cargo of furs would sell for more in East Asia than it would in Saint Louis or New York.

Astor's American Fur Company and the Pacific Fur Company launched expeditions across the Louisiana Territory to Oregon. His company also used sea routes from New York, around Cape Horn, and up the Pacific coast. In March 1811, the overland expedition reached Oregon and began construction on a settlement called Astoria. The business of fur trading started immediately. The Astorians established trading posts on the Columbia and Snake Rivers. The men explored present-day Oregon, Washington, and Idaho and returned to Astoria with otter and beaver pelts.

In 1812, several Astorians, led by Robert Stuart, set out from Oregon to meet with Astor in Saint Louis. As they made their way east, the group discovered a route that ran south of the original Lewis and Clark expedition's route. One day, this would become the Oregon Trail.

Stuart and his men also found a 20-mile- (32-km-) wide pass that ran through the Rocky Mountains. Unlike other passes through the Rocky Mountains, this one was a gentle slope rather than a

Not Fit for Farming

In 1819, the government hired Stephen H. Long, an explorer and a map-maker. He journeyed west from Nebraska, through Iowa, to the Rocky Mountains, Oklahoma, and Arkansas. He made maps of various areas, including an area known today as the Great American Plains. He labeled it the Great American Desert. At that time, desert was used in the sense that the land was dry and had few trees. Long deemed the land unsuitable for those who depended on agriculture.

steep, mountainous drop-off. This was the only place where wagons could easily travel across the mountain range. What became known as the South Pass would one day make the trip to Oregon much easier for emigrants.

However, the South Pass was forgotten for many years after stories circulated about the Great American Desert, which was the name given to the prairie lands in the central regions of the Louisiana Territory. Because there was little water or shade in these grasslands, explorers dismissed this overland route to Oregon as impractical and dangerous.

In 1822, Jedediah Smith answered an advertisement placed by General William Henry Ashley, lieutenant governor of Missouri, seeking men for an expedition:

> *To Enterprising young men: The subscriber wishes to engage one hundred men, to ascend the river Missouri to its source, there to be employed for one, two or three years.*[1]

When the expedition up the Missouri River failed, Ashley sent his men west to the Rockies to find an overland route. In 1823, Smith and his men came to the South Pass through the Rockies, proving that the mountains were not the barrier they were thought to be. Many of the men who traveled in these expeditions, such as Smith, Jim Bridger, and Jim Beckwourth, became the legendary mountain men who blazed trails west.

ADVENTURERS AND EXPEDITIONS

Increasing numbers of trappers and traders made their way toward what would become Oregon—despite the threat of some

Jedediah Smith and the Bear

On an expedition to find alternate routes through the Rocky Mountains, mountain man Jedediah Smith was attacked by a grizzly bear. The bear not only broke several of Smith's ribs, it seized Smith's entire head in its mouth and tore off most of one ear. One young trapper in Smith's expedition did what he could to help, as he later wrote:

I asked [Smith] what was best. He said, "One or two go for water and if you have a needle and thread get it out and sew up my wounds around my head". . . . One of his ears was torn from his head out to the outer rim. After stitching all the other wounds in the best way I was capable and according to the captain's directions, the ear being the last, I told him I could do nothing for his ear. "Oh, you must try to stitch it up some way or other," said he. Then I put in my needle and stitched . . . the lacerated parts together as nice as I could with my hands. . . . This gave us a lesson on the character of the grizzly bear which we did not forget.[2]

Mountain Men

Several mountain men who roamed the Rockies during the days before the Oregon Trail later became famous for other reasons. Kit Carson, a legend of the old West, served as a scout and guide for John Charles Frémont's 1842 expeditions to map the Oregon Trail. Years later, Carson became known for his role in driving the Navajo out of Arizona in 1864 in what has been called the "long walk" to a reservation in New Mexico. Navajos were forced to walk from their Arizona reservation to the eastern part of New Mexico.

Jim Bridger, another mountain man, was a trapper, trader, guide, merchant, Indian interpreter, and army officer. He was the first Euro-American man to view the Great Salt Lake in what is now Utah. He also found what became known as Bridger's Pass, which was a shorter route through the Rocky Mountains than the South Pass.

hostile Native American tribes. Many of the trappers were adventurers. They dressed in animal skins and survived by living off the land rather than bringing supplies with them. These mountain men roamed throughout the West—often with Native American companions. The men learned more about the western lands, and some would later guide settlers along the trail to Oregon.

More trading posts and settlements were being created in the West. In 1825, John McLoughlin established the Fort Vancouver trading post for the Hudson Bay Company in Oregon Country. Slowly, the area was settled by fur trappers, traders, and their families, setting the stage for the influx of Americans.

Beginning in 1832, Captain Benjamin Bonneville was on leave from the US Army, but he carried out an expedition for the federal

Mountain men of the West as depicted by Frederic Remington

government to chart the land. New York financier Alfred Seton paid for the expedition. Bonneville traveled across the Rocky Mountains with a company of 110 soldiers. With his group of 20 wagons, he was credited for taking the first wagons across the Rocky Mountains summit at the South Pass, crossing the Continental Divide.

The Continental Divide

The Continental Divide in the United States determines where the flow of water (except for some rivers) drains. Precipitation on the east side of the divide flows to the Atlantic Ocean or the Gulf of Mexico. Precipitation on the west side of the divide flows to the Pacific Ocean. The divide runs north to south. Every continent except Antarctica has a continental divide.

More expeditions followed. Nathaniel Wyeth from Boston, Massachusetts, was interested in the stories of western rivers teeming with fish. In 1832, he led the first party of American settlers to Oregon overland. Wanting to establish a fishing business, he hired William Sublette, an explorer, trapper, trader, and mountain man, to guide him and his group to Oregon. When Wyeth found that the stories of fish in Oregon were true, he returned to Boston to purchase the equipment for his new company. He went back to Oregon in 1834 and established the Fort Hall outpost. It later became a landmark and supply post on the Oregon Trail.

THE WHITMAN PARTY

In 1836, a group of missionaries traveled west to Fort Vancouver. Missionaries Narcissa Whitman and Eliza Spalding became the first Euro-American women to cross the Rocky Mountains. The group was the first to take their wagons all the way to Oregon. Previous expeditions had left their wagons in present-day Idaho for fear the wagons were not strong enough to cross the mountains. The Whitman party proved it was possible to travel to Oregon by wagon.

THE SUBLETTE CUTOFF

In 1844, Sublette found a shortcut that became an alternate route on the Oregon Trail. The cutoff trimmed 45 to 50 miles (72–80 km)—approximately three days of travel—from the traditional Oregon Trail route. However, the decision to take it was always risky.

What became known as the Sublette Cutoff crossed an arid landscape with desert heat and little available water or grass. Taking the cutoff risked the death of the animals that pulled the wagons. Those who did take the cutoff often preferred to travel by night, leaving camp at 2:00 a.m. to travel in the cool darkness and limit exposure to the daytime

Narcissa Whitman

The story of Narcissa Whitman and her party is not a happy one. Marcus Whitman led a wagon train to Oregon. He and his wife took in 11 orphaned children of emigrants, including the Sager children. After traveling to Oregon, the Whitmans and the Spaldings, another missionary couple, established a mission in present-day Washington. They attempted to minister to the Cayuse tribes. However, after an epidemic of measles killed many Cayuse children, the Cayuse blamed the missionaries. They massacred 14 people, including the Whitmans, and burned the mission buildings in November 1847.

heat. Young boys carried lanterns and walked ahead of the wagons to light the way. The cutoff was wide enough for the wagons to travel side by side and not follow in the dust of a wagon ahead of them.

The stage was set for the great influx of emigrants on the Oregon Trail. Facing an economic depression, desperate and adventurous people were looking for a fresh start—and they were willing to risk everything to achieve it. ⌐

Sublette Cutoff

The Sublette Cutoff received its heaviest traffic during the Gold Rush of the 1840s and 1850s when a guidebook mentioned the route, which convinced as many as 20,000 travelers to follow it.

*Narcissa Whitman, a member of the Whitman missionary expedition,
helping an ill Native American*

Andrew Jackson was president of the United States during the Panic of 1837.

MANIFEST DESTINY

The Panic of 1837 began a depression that lasted for several years and was a difficult time for the United States. Farmers received less money for their crops than it cost to grow them, and many lost their farms when they were unable to pay back their bank loans. Banks restricted credit. Small businesses that relied on purchases from farmers also went bankrupt. Food riots occurred in large cities. Railroad and canal construction projects were canceled as contractors were unable to pay for them. Unemployment was widespread.

In this economic climate, the idea of moving to Oregon and making a fresh start was appealing. Americans had read and heard about Oregon for many years as various expeditions traveled there. With little left for them at home, many decided to pack up and go west.

The First Wagons

The Whitman party had proved that it was possible to travel by wagon to Oregon. In 1842, Elijah J. White led approximately 100 people to Oregon following the trail the Whitmans had taken. White was the first official sent by the US government into Oregon Country. As an Indian agent, White was responsible for all dealings between settlers and Native Americans, which included the Nez Perce, Cayuse, and Walla Walla.

During part of the journey, White's wagon train was led by a former mountain man, Thomas "Broken

Beyond Endurance

The decision to emigrate was almost always made by the men of a family. For most women, the thought of leaving their homes was agonizing and painful. Not every woman dutifully followed her husband to Oregon. The difficulties of the trail often pushed women beyond endurance. Chores such as laundry, gathering wood, and cooking were done outdoors—regardless of the weather or if they were pregnant. A journal entry tells of one woman who did not want to continue the trip:

"September 15th. Laid by. This morning our company moved on, except one family. The woman got mad and wouldn't budge or let the children go. He had the cattle hitched on for three hours and coaxed her to go, but she wouldn't stir. [Several men] went and each one took a young one and crammed them in the wagon and the husband drove off and left her sitting."[1]

Hand" Fitzpatrick. Beavers were no longer plentiful in parts of the West due to overtrapping. Men such as Fitzpatrick could no longer survive on hunting and trapping. Instead, these men found they could make money using their expertise with the western landscape to guide groups of emigrants to Oregon.

That same year, the US government sent John Charles Frémont, a young army officer, to the West, specifically to explore and map the territory of the Oregon Trail. Frémont made several trips to the Oregon and California regions, mapping the areas he traveled through while collecting plant and animal specimens. He wrote books about his expeditions with the help of his wife, Jessie. His descriptions made people eager to emigrate to the West.

Because the US government had sent Frémont and a military team

*John Charles Frémont explored and mapped
the territory of the Oregon Trail.*

to map the area, it convinced many people that the
United States intended to make Oregon Country,
which was occupied by the British, part of the United
States. The Oregon Treaty, signed in 1846, ended
the dispute. A border was established between what
is now called British Columbia and the states of
Washington, Idaho, and Montana.

Stories about the Oregon Territory began to
create "Oregon fever" as the accounts of trappers
and missionaries, government reports, letters from
new settlers, and descriptions from travelers fed

As Oregon fever swept the country, societies formed to encourage Americans to travel westward and settle in Oregon. Some of these societies wanted to Christianize the Native Americans.

The New England Emigrant Aid Company was formed by a group of abolitionists from New Hampshire who traveled to Kansas. Their goal was to fight for a free Kansas.

The Oregon Provisional Emigration Society was formed by Methodist ministers and church members. This society published the *Oregonian* to convince easterners to emigrate. In 1840, the society organized a large wagon train to travel to the West. The *Oregonian* provided information and assured potential travelers that "Christian settlers would go with the gospel of peace and love to help the Indians, who were certain to recognize such beneficent motives and respond accordingly."[2]

people's imaginations. Oregon offered rich soil, few epidemics of disease, and plenty of space. In an effort to persuade families and individuals to join emigrant wagon trains westward, formal and informal lectures and presentations were given in many towns in the East. Oregon societies were formed, attracting members who would pledge to migrate west. Some people did not need much persuading:

> *Mr. Burnett hauled a box out on to the sidewalk, took his stand upon it, and began to tell us about the land flowing with milk and honey on the shores of the Pacific . . . he told of great crops of wheat which it was possible to raise in Oregon, and . . . the richness of the soil and . . . with a little twinkle in his eye he said "and they do say gentlemen, that out in Oregon the pigs are running about under the great acorn trees, round and fat, and already cooked, with knives and forks*

sticking in them so that you can cut off a slice whenever you are hungry."... Father was so moved by what he heard... that he decided to join the company that was going west to Oregon... Father was the first to sign his name.[3]

THE GREAT MIGRATION

By 1843, the trickle of emigrants traveling to the West had become a surge—the Great Migration had begun. In the towns of Independence and Saint Joseph, Missouri, thousands of people gathered to begin the trip westward. These towns became known as jumping-off points. If a person or family did not belong to a group forming a wagon train, they joined one there. Emigrants purchased the necessary supplies for their trips, including wagons and food. Some wagon trains hired men to hunt buffalo to supply meat for the emigrants.

MANIFEST DESTINY

The term *manifest destiny* was first used by journalist John L. O'Sullivan in an article in the *United States Magazine and Democratic Review* in 1845. He favored westward expansion and wrote that it was "our manifest destiny to overspread the continent allotted by Providence for the free development of our multiplying millions."[4] O'Sullivan believed Americans had the God-given right to settle and control the entire continent from the Atlantic coast to the Pacific coast, regardless of who (Native Americans, Spanish, those of mixed ethnicity, etc.) had claimed the land. Many other Americans held the same belief.

Many of the people traveling west had no real idea of what the trek would be like. Some had read guidebooks such

Buy the Book

As more people began to travel the trails, the publishing and sale of trail guidebooks, which sold for as little as ten cents, became a lucrative business. Lansford Warren Hastings's guidebook, *The Emigrants' Guide to Oregon and California*, was popular. However, not every guidebook was accurate. Some had been written from a person's recollection or from stories they had heard. Information was inaccurate regarding landmarks. Some emigrants were misled into taking dangerous cutoffs or routes.

In the winter of 1846–1847, a well-equipped wagon train headed for California. Upon arriving at the Little Sandy River, a disagreement occurred. Jacob Donner and James Reed wanted to follow the route Hastings described even though it had not been traveled by a wagon train. Mountain man James Clyman had used the Hastings cutoff and advised the group against it. Still, the Donner-Reed party followed the shortcut.

Unfortunately, Hastings had never seen the cutoff or traveled on it. His directions led the Donner-Reed party into a rugged area of the Sierra Nevada Mountains. The passes were blocked by snow; the party was trapped without enough supplies to last the winter. When the rescuers arrived, 46 of 87 people in the group had died.

as *The Emigrants' Guide to Oregon and California*, written in 1845 by Lansford Warren Hastings. It listed the necessary supplies and provided information that might be helpful to emigrants:

CHAPTER XV.
THE EQUIPMENT, SUPPLIES,
AND THE METHOD OF TRAVELING.

Equipment; kinds of arms; quantity of ammunition. Supplies; quantity of provisions; kinds of. Buffalo, not depended upon. Advisable to drive cattle. Cooking utensils; few to be taken. Beds; kind of, preferred. Horses preferred, for the saddle. Mules preferable for the harness. Oxen preferred to horses or mules. Working cows; not advised. . . . What horses and mules to be shod. Additional supplies; what to be taken. Method of traveling. Place of rendezvous; time of arriving at; time of departure from. . . . Nocturnal encampment. Method of guarding camp; of guarding herds. Territory of hostile Indians; extent of; method of traveling in. Defensive attitude; method of assuming. Horses, not turned out. Day and night guards; duty of. Fires extinguished. Elk in human form. Indians mimicing wolves. Guns carried loaded, but not capped or primed. Horses in chase of buffalo without riders. Large companies objectionable. Difficulties and dangers avoidable. [5]

Only some of the guidebooks were accurate. Others provided incorrect routes and landmarks, which led to delays and even tragedy. The year 1843 marked the beginning of more than two decades of migration in a land of opportunity. In 1843, approximately 875 emigrants made the trip westward. In 1847, the migration number grew to 4,000. Between 1843 and 1869, approximately 500,000 people had migrated. But it was one thing to dream of a new life in Oregon and quite another to travel 2,000 miles (3,200 km) from a Missouri River jumping-off point to reach it.

Buffalo hunters provided meat for some wagon trains on the Oregon Trail.

Members of a wagon train bought supplies at a jumping-off point.

ON THE TRAIL

O nce the decision had been made to head
for Oregon, the emigrants were at the
beginning of a long trail that would be mentally
and physically exhausting. The territory west of
the Missouri River was vast and unfamiliar, but the

emigrants would travel along what had become an established trail with landmarks and stopping-off points. Much like modern road maps of highways, the emigrants followed a series of directions they hoped would lead them safely to Oregon.

Jumping Off

The first step along the trail to Oregon was a jumping-off point. This is where wagon trains assembled and emigrants accumulated the necessary supplies and animals needed for the trip. The most famous and popular jumping-off point was the town of Independence, Missouri. Farther up the Missouri River, towns such as Westport, Saint Joseph, Omaha, and Council Bluffs were also used as staging points. These previously small and quiet towns had become boomtowns, bustling with activity and doing a huge business in equipment to outfit the wagon trains.

The optimal time for starting the westward trip was during the last two weeks of April. By then, the prairie grass had grown enough to provide

"A multitude of shops had sprung up to furnish emigrants . . . with necessaries for the journey. . . there was an incessant hammering and banging from a dozen blacksmiths' sheds, where the heavy wagons were being repaired, and the horses and oxen shod. The streets were thronged with men, horses, and mules."[1]

—*Emigrant and historian Francis Parkman*

grazing for the animals of the wagon train. As the best departure days approached, the prairie just outside Independence was crowded with the wagons of emigrants. When it was time to start the journey, the congestion was so severe that traffic jams of wagons and animals developed. This was worsened by the people in the wagons who were fresh from city life and did not know how to yoke or drive a team of oxen or mules. They bumped their wagons into trees or tipped them over. Many experienced difficulties in getting their animals to proceed in the right direction.

GETTING STARTED

Whether the emigrants started from Independence or other towns along the Missouri River, they all traveled across the Great Plains. The trail led farther northwest across a corner of what is now Kansas and into Nebraska. The emigrants encountered the prairie of thick grasses that grew taller than a man. It tangled in the wagon wheels, and young children could easily become lost in it.

As the wagons crossed Kansas and Nebraska, many rivers presented obstacles. Some could be forded, but others required the use of canoes to float wagons across or the use of a toll bridge. At times, this led to tragedy when wagons capsized and family members drowned.

The Platte River, called the Big Muddy by emigrants, was a treacherous river. In June, when most emigrants crossed it, the river was a series of shallow, stagnant pools connected by mudflats, sandbars, and a channel three feet (0.9 m) deep. Wagons followed a path of willow poles that marked the sandbars in the riverbed that would support the weight.

THE HIGH PRAIRIE

As the travelers followed the Platte River, the landscape became drier and more open as the tall prairie grass was

A Mind of Their Own

According to John Hawkins Clark who tried to cross the Missouri River in 1852:

The Missouri River has to be crossed to-day. . . our progress was very slow for as we got one mule on board and our attention directed to another the first one would jump overboard and swim ashore, to the great delight of the many who were looking on. After several turns of the kind, . . . we concluded to drive them all on together. In this we succeeded admirably, for on they went and we put up the railing to keep them there. A shout of victory followed . . . and the order given to "cast-off," but before the order could be obeyed the fiends in mule shape took it into their heads to look over the same side of the boat and all at the same time. Result, the dipping of the boat to the water's edge on one side, which frightened the little brutes themselves and they all, as with common consent, leaped overboard again.[2]

Chimney Rock is a famous landmark above the North Platte River valley along the Oregon Trail.

replaced by the low grass of the High Plains. The Oto and Ponca were peaceful Native Americans who farmed and hunted along rivers.

The Pawnee farmed beans, corn, and squash and hunted buffalo on the plains. Although the Pawnee fought with other Native American tribes, they were not hostile to the settlers.

Emigrants now saw prairie dog towns and herds of buffalo. Spectacular sandstone formations along the river became landmarks: Courthouse Rock, Jail

Rock, and Chimney Rock could be seen from a distance that was three days away. A. J. McCall, an emigrant describing Chimney Rock in 1849, said that before they reached it, the solitary rock looked like "an old ruin, then a very sharp cone, more the shape of a chimney than anything else."[3]

After reaching Fort Laramie in Wyoming, the emigrants passed Register Cliff, a sandstone formation where many signed their names or left messages for other travelers. As the trail continued through the soft sandstone of Wyoming, the wagon wheels that gouged into the soft stone left ruts that still can be seen today.

Starting in the early spring, migrants hoped to make it to Independence Rock by July 4, which is how the well-known landmark got its name. The rock was big enough to cover five acres (2 ha) of prairie. Because of the good grass for grazing

Independence Rock

Many emigrants who stopped at Independence Rock wrote their names on it, continuing a tradition begun by the trappers and mountain men who came before them. Some carved their names, but the rock was much harder than the sandstone cliffs at Register Cliff. Others wrote their names using axle grease, which was made from pine tar or hog fat.

In 1860, traveler Sir Richard Burton estimated between 40,000 and 50,000 names were written on Independence Rock. In certain sheltered areas of the rock, some of these names are visible today.

Joseph Williams

In the spring of 1841, Joseph Williams, an itinerant preacher, embarked on the Oregon Trail. Like many travelers, he kept a journal of his trip:

"April 26th, 1841. This morning I started from my residence, near Napoleon, Ripley County, Indiana, for the Oregon Territory on the Columbia River, west of the Rocky Mountains; though many of my friends tried to dissuade me from going, telling me of the many dangers and difficulties I should have to go through, exposed to hostile Indians and the wild beasts, and also on account of my advanced age, being at this time in my 64th year. But my mind leads me strongly to go; I want to preach to the people there, and also to the Indians, as well as to see the country."[4]

in the area, most wagon trains stopped there. This was another place where emigrants wrote their names. Shortly past Independence Rock, the travelers came to the halfway point on the Oregon Trail: South Pass. The next portion of the journey was to cross the Rocky Mountains.

FOLLOWING THE SNAKE

Once the emigrants made it across the Rockies, the trail moved northwest toward the Snake River. They traveled through Idaho, passing an area of lava features such as geysers and hot springs. In the territory of trappers and mountain men, the emigrants reached Fort Hall, which was older than the trail.

At Three Island Crossing, the emigrant wagons crossed the Snake River and entered the lush green Boise River valley. The emigrants stopped at Fort Boise, which was built in 1834. Beyond the adobe

Emigrants forded the Snake River at Three Island Crossing.

Fort Boise, the trail finally entered Oregon. The wagons climbed up and over the Blue Mountains with its heavy stands of timber and steep grades that were difficult for tired animals to cross. Once over these mountains, the trail crossed several tributaries of the Columbia River before reaching the Cascade Mountains.

During its earliest years, the Oregon Trail ended at Dalles, Oregon, where emigrants had to take the dangerous Columbia River route to the Willamette valley. Lydia Allen Rudd, who emigrated to Oregon in 1852, wrote of traveling down the river in a canoe:

> *It was now getting dark and the wind increasing . . . the waves washed over the canoe and as high as my head completely drenching us with water. [The Native American men] then tried to make for the shore but were unable to manage the canoe but fortunately there was more oars on the boat and our men assisted all they could. And after a long time we safely made the shore which was more than we expected. Glad to lay down on the sand in our wet clothes and on our wet bed. One lady was very much alarmed screaming every breath as loud as she possibly could. A sorry time.* [5]

The land route was blocked by the steep, heavily forested mountains of the Cascade Range. After 1846, wagons followed the Barlow Road and skirted Mount Hood before descending into the Willamette valley. At a distance of not quite 2,000 miles (3,219 km) from Independence, Missouri, weary emigrants camped in a large meadow called Abernathy Green close to Oregon City. Their journey was over.

Independence Rock was one of the milestones of the Oregon Trail.

*The death of oxen often meant the emigrants carried
what they could and walked the trail.*

LIFE IN A WAGON TRAIN

The trail from Missouri to Oregon was not
only challenging and dangerous but often fatal
for the emigrants who traveled it. Apart from the
larger issues of following the trail, those making the
journey also faced survival on a day-by-day basis.

Stocking Up

Emigrants packed up their lives to move to a new place, but they also needed enough supplies to survive for as many as five or six months on the trail. A family of four needed as much as 1,000 pounds (454 kg) of food just to survive the journey. A team of oxen and a wagon were needed to pull the weight. Emigrants used oxen because horses did not survive well on prairie grass along the trail. Oxen were strong and could survive on the many plants that grew wild.

There were no roads, only trails. Because of the length and condition of the trails, emigrants did not use the heavy Conestoga wagons that carried freight in the eastern United States. Pulling a wagon of that size could kill a team of six oxen, leaving their passengers stranded on the trail.

Instead, the emigrants used smaller and lighter farm wagons, which oxen could pull. The wagons were outfitted with a canvas cover that was pulled tightly shut over the openings to keep out dust. In an attempt to keep items dry, the canvas or cotton

A Noble Animal

Emigrant Peter Burnett noted:

"The ox is a most noble animal, patient, thrifty, durable, gentle and does not run off. . . . The ox will plunge through mud, swim over streams, dive into thickets and he will eat almost anything."[1]

covers were treated with linseed oil. These classic covered wagons were known as prairie schooners.

The front wheels of these wagons could pivot, making turns easier. The wagon box carried food, tools, and only what was considered necessary. Still, a packed four feet by ten feet (1.2 m by 3 m) wagon box carried as much as 1.25 tons (1.13 t) of cargo. This weight was supported by massive axles. Sometimes, an axle on the wagon broke, forcing the emigrants to use the parts to make a two-wheeled cart and carry what they could.

Once the emigrants had a

Just Another Day

Sunday, May 8th—Sunday morning. Still in camp waiting to cross. There are three hundred or more wagons in sight and as far as the eye can reach, the bottom is covered, on each side of the river, with cattle and horses. There is not ferry here and the men will have to make one out of the tightest wagon-bed (every company should have a waterproof wagon-bed for this purpose). Everything must now be hauled out of the wagons head over heels (and he who knows where to find anything will be a smart fellow), then the wagons must be all taken to pieces, and then by means of a strong rope stretched across the river, with a tight wagon-bed attached to the middle of it, the rope must be long enough to pull from one side to the other, with men on each side of the river to pull it. In this way we have to cross everything a little at a time. Women and children last, and then swim the cattle and horses. There were three horses and some cattle drowned while crossing this place yesterday.[2]

—Amelia Stewart Knight, 1853

wagon and two to four oxen, they needed to gather the necessary supplies for the trip. Some families took a cow along for fresh milk and butter. Most brought staples such as beans, rice, and hardtack, which was dried bread that had to be softened in water to be eaten.

In his guide, Hastings also advised against taking too many kitchen utensils, suggesting that only a frying pan, coffee pot, baking kettle, tin cups, plates, and eating utensils were necessary. Some emigrants loaded furniture in their wagons—only to leave it by the side of the trail when they realized the extra weight was a luxury they could no longer carry. Extra parts for wagons, tools for repairs, and basic medical supplies were a necessity, although some wagon trains included a doctor to handle illnesses and injuries.

Once the emigrants were outfitted, they joined up with a wagon

A Pioneer Travel Trailer

Some pioneer wagons could be cozy and convenient on the trail. One emigrant's recollections included a description of a family's kitchen on wheels:

"On the center crosspiece [of the wagon] was placed a little round sheet-metal stove, about the size of a three-gallon [11 L] bucket, with a little tea-kettle, a boiler and frying pan. On this little stove cooking was done with great ease and satisfaction. . . . On cold nights their little stove made their house very comfortable. They also had a little churn in the kitchen. The milk was placed in the churn each morning and the motion of the wagon churned it, so that every evening they had fresh butter."[3]

*Emigrants often had to leave items by the side of
the trail to lighten a wagon's load.*

train. Hired guides often led the wagon train on the
trail; elected officials governed the group. A wagon
train might consist of as few as four or five wagons
and, in some cases, as many as 120. Some wagon
trains were assembled with friends and neighbors
who wished to travel together, but others might
consist of strangers who joined together at jumping-
off points such as Independence.

A Day on the Trail

Once the emigrants set off, many faced a 2,000-mile (3,219-km) walk because there was no room to ride in the overloaded wagons. Life settled into a routine of traveling all day and camping at night. A signal was given to awaken the group before sunrise. The travelers started their day with a quick breakfast of leftover cold food or cooked food before taking down tents and yoking the oxen. Those who were not ready to leave when the wagon leader gave the signal found themselves at the end of the train.

Playing on the Trail

Like children anywhere, those who traveled along the Oregon Trail found ways to keep themselves entertained. They even found a way to make a toy much like the modern plastic Frisbee—only this one was made of buffalo dung. The buffalo chips left by herds of buffalo on the prairie were flat, round, and very hard once they had dried in the sun. The children tossed these back and forth before the chips became part of the evening fire.

The wagons and animals ahead of them created clouds of dust or churned wet ground into mud. Several men rode ahead of the train as scouts to look for landmarks and to warn the wagons of any upcoming hazards. These men also hunted to supply fresh meat for the travelers. The emigrants took a break at noon before continuing the journey.

By 6:00 p.m., it was time to set up camp for the night. The wagons were usually arranged into a circle to create a corral to hold livestock. The women gathered wood to start their campfires then cooked over an open fire. This was a challenge as staples such as bread could not easily be baked over a fire and often was burnt on the outside and raw on the inside. Keeping bugs and dirt out of food was another challenge. Finding fuel for campfires became more difficult. As the trail became more heavily traveled, accessible wood became scarce. Emigrants learned to use buffalo chips—the dried manure from herds of buffalo—for fires.

As night fell, the emigrants slept beneath their wagons, in tents, directly on the ground, or sometimes inside their wagons. Awake at sunrise, they continued the routine. At best, they hoped to cover 15 to 20 miles (24–32 km) of trail each day. When possible, they observed the Sabbath, but it was not a day of rest. They used the day to wash clothes and repair equipment.

Life was not all hardship and work, however. In the evenings, fiddle and harmonica music filled the air, and emigrants who had brought books might read aloud to others. Children ran and played together. Some single men and women met, courted, and married along the trail. ⌐

In Remington's illustration, a scout signals to
a wagon train that there is water.

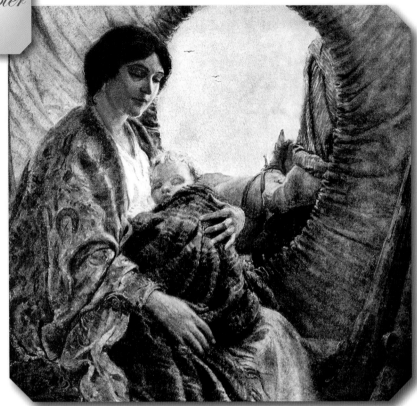

Births and deaths were common during the westward migration.

Dangers on the Trail

migrants traveling across the vast expanses of the western United States were far from help if an emergency should arise. And emergencies happened frequently on the trail, leaving the travelers to cope the best they could.

INJURIES AND ILLNESSES

Death was common on the Oregon Trail. Accidents occurred in the blink of an eye. Children fell beneath the heavy wagons and were crushed. Ferries overturned and people drowned. At times, wagons broke loose and tumbled down steep inclines. Catherine Sager Pringle was injured during her trip west as a child:

> We had by this time got used to climbing in and out of the wagon when in motion. When performing this feat that afternoon my dress caught on an axle [handle] and I was thrown under the wagon wheel, which passed over and badly crushed my limb before father could stop the team. He picked me up and saw the extent of the injury when the injured limb hung dangling in the air.[1]

Many of the women traveling on the Oregon Trail were of childbearing age and were pregnant or gave birth during the trip. Often, the women and newborn babies did not survive the trip. In her book, *Women's Diaries of the Westward Journey*, Lillian Schlissel wrote of the hazards facing these women:

> For women who were pregnant, the overland crossing could be a nightmare. One never knew for certain where labor might begin: in Indian Territory, or in the mountains, or in

drenching rain. One might be alone, with no women to help, and only fear at hand. The birth might be simple, or it might be complicated and tortuous.[2]

The trail was also a place where illness could easily incapacitate or kill a family member. The biggest killer was cholera, a disease that was not widely understood at the time. This contagious bacterial disease affects the intestines. Contaminated food or water was often its source. Cholera killed more emigrants than anything else on the trail. Cholera could spread so quickly that a healthy man might become infected and die within just a few hours.

DEALING WITH THE DEAD

Because death was common on the Oregon Trail, the route was soon marked by many graves. Wood was often scarce, so there were no coffins. The dead were wrapped in canvas and buried. Rocks might be piled on top of the graves for protection. Stopping too long on the trail to bury their loved ones could strand wagon trains in the snow of the mountain passes. Little time was allowed to perform funerals for those who died. Due to the fear of being stranded, along with the knowledge that anyone who suffered from cholera would not survive long, some were left by the side of the trail before they died.

Some graves had headstones, but others were unmarked fearing that Native Americans or other travelers might dig them up and scavenge the bodies. Animals were also known to disturb graves and scatter the bones. Sometimes, graves were dug on the trail itself so that the wagons would travel over them and obscure any signs. Agnes Stewart wrote about a grave she had seen:

Joel Hembree

The earliest-known grave on the Oregon Trail is that of six-year-old Joel Hembree. He died on July 18, 1843, when he slipped under the wheels of a wagon and his abdomen was crushed. Joel was buried and his grave marked with a stone.

The grave was forgotten until 1961. While collecting rocks, the owner of the property turned over a flat rock that revealed the inscription. Because a new dam was being constructed, Joel's body was moved. His bones, which were perfectly preserved, had been laid on a bed of branches and covered by an oak dresser drawer. The original gravestone was placed at the new grave.

We camped at a place where a woman had been buried and the wolves dug her up. Her hair was there with a comb still in it. She had been buried too shallow. It seems a dreadful fate, but what is the difference? One cannot feel after the spirit is flown.[4]

Emigrant Francis Parkman recalled,

One morning, a piece of plank, standing upright on the summit of a grassy hill . . . we found the following words very roughly traced upon it, apparently with a red–hot piece of iron:

Mary Ellis
Died May 7th 1845 Aged two months.[5]

WILD WEATHER

Weather was another source of hardship and danger for the emigrants. Many were not accustomed to the strong thunderstorms that occurred on the plains with heavy rain, high winds, lightning strikes, and hail. When it rained, there was no shelter other than a leaky wagon. The rain also turned the trail to mud. Creeks and rivers swollen with rainwater were difficult to cross and often forced the wagon train to delay for days or even weeks before moving on.

Emigrants who left too late in the season were more likely to encounter brutal cold and

Emigrants made camp during the winter.

snow toward the end of the trail, especially in mountainous regions. Heavy snows could trap emigrants in the mountains until spring with insufficient supplies. At best, snow, mud, and cold made travel difficult as the Donner-Reed party found in 1846 to 1847. Elizabeth Smith Geer described what she experienced in 1847:

> *It rains and snows, . . . I carry my babe and lead, or rather carry, another through snow mud and water, almost to my knees. It is the worst road. . . . I went ahead with my children*

and I was afraid to look behind me for fear of seeing the wagon turn over into the mud. . . . I have not told you half we suffered. I am not adequate to the task.[6]

Meek's Cutoff

Stephen Meek was a trapper and a guide for wagon parties. He dreamed of finding a cutoff that would eliminate the need for the dangerous water journey down the Columbia River.

In 1845, Meek met a party of several hundred wagons on their way to the Willamette valley. Rumors had spread that the Walla Walla and Cayuse might attack settlers on the usual route through the Blue Mountains of Oregon or along the Columbia River. Meek told the emigrants he knew of a cutoff that was an old Indian trail across the Blue and Cascade Mountains. He promised that his cutoff would bring them to the valley weeks before anyone taking the river route.

Meek, however, had never traveled on this trail; he had only heard rumors of it. Approximately 200 wagons followed him into a rocky and dry landscape with little water. It soon became apparent that Meek did not know where he was as he led the wagons on a meandering trail. Angry train members talked about lynching Meek, but they stuck together. Eventually, they made it back to Dalles, 40 days behind the other members of their wagon train who had taken the river route. Seventy-five members of "Meek's Terrible Cutoff" group died. Meek and his wife went into hiding to avoid the angry travelers.

FRIENDS AND ENEMIES

Another danger on the trail, but often exaggerated in emigration guides, was that of the Native American tribes. The trail passed through the territories of many tribes including the Pawnee and Cheyenne. Most interactions between the emigrants and Native Americans were peaceful and even beneficial. The Native Americans often helped emigrants by rounding up stray animals, rescuing travelers, or helping free wagons that had become stuck. Emigrants traded with tribe members for food or horses by offering clothing, rifles, or tobacco in exchange.

As the traffic increased and the supplies of firewood, prairie grass, and buffalo were depleted, some Native Americans began to fight back against the emigrant invasion. US government policies such as the Indian Removal Act of 1830 and dwindling territory made the tribes hostile to the settlers. Some emigrants and Native Americans were killed. Some emigrants went out of their way to take routes to avoid areas known to be dangerous.

However, many travelers found that the lurid accounts of massacres were overstated. Amelia Stewart Knight, writing from the trail in

A Cow and a War

In September 1854, one of the worst incidents between emigrants and Native Americans occurred. The outcome of this seemingly small event reveals a great deal about the longer, ongoing struggle that was taking shape between the United States and Native Americans.

It all began when a cow wandered away from a wagon train and into a Lakota camp where it was butchered for food. The cow may have been alive and returned if its owners had asked earlier. Instead, they went to Fort Laramie and told US Army Lieutenant John Lawrence Grattan the story of the "stolen" cow. Grattan took 29 soldiers with him to punish the tribe. Conquering Bear, the Lakota chief, offered to replace the now-dead cow with a horse. This was more than a fair trade, but Grattan ordered his men to fire. In the attack and retaliation, the chief and 85 other Lakota were killed—all because of a cow.

1853 from a place where emigrants have been known to be killed, noted,

> *I was very much frightened while at this camp. I lay awake all night. I expected every minute we would be killed. However, we all found our scalps on in the morning.*[7]

In 1854, the Shoshone massacred 18 emigrants along the Snake River; two emigrants managed to escape. The event has become known as the Ward Massacre. This was the first massacre along the Snake River.

From 1840 to 1860, an estimated 362 emigrants were killed by Native Americans. During the same timeframe, approximately 426 Native Americans were killed by emigrants. More emigrants died from accident or disease than from hostile Native Americans. Estimates of deaths by disease or accidents range from 20,000 to 30,000 deaths along the 2,000 miles (3,219 km) of trail or approximately 10 to 15 deaths every mile (1.6 km).

Despite the hardships and dangers of the trail, an estimated 350,000 people emigrated along the Oregon Trail from 1841 to 1866. Events would soon swell the waves of emigrants to a flood.

*This marker commemorates those who made
the journey on the Oregon Trail.*

This map shows the Oregon and Mormon Trails.

A Home in the West

After the Great Migration of 1843, thousands traveled the trail every year—as many as 55,000 in 1850. However, circumstances beyond the desire for a better life in Oregon motivated more people to move across the country.

THE MORMON INFLUENCE

Joseph Smith came from a large family of 11 children. Born in Vermont in December 1805, Joseph was the fifth child. The poor farming family moved to New York in search of better farmland. He had little formal education, but he did learn to read and write.

In 1820, in Palmyra, New York, 14-year-old Joseph had a revelation that he was to prepare himself for greater work that lay ahead. A later revelation directed him to dig up plates of gold that were inscribed with sacred history. After translating the tablets, Smith published the *Book of Mormon* in 1830 and founded a new church known as the Church of Jesus Christ of Latter-Day Saints.

As the religion grew from six members to several hundred in the first year, Smith decreed that his church was intended to create a new city in the West. As he and his followers moved to Ohio and then to Missouri, they were increasingly unwelcomed and even threatened. Geoffrey C. Ward wrote about the Mormons in his book *The West*:

> *Missouri clergymen denounced their faith. Missouri settlers feared their growing numbers. Rumors spread that they*

were stealing, stirring up the Indians, planning to free the slaves, printing counterfeit money. "The Mormons," one Presbyterian minister told his flock, "are the common enemies of mankind and ought to be destroyed." Smith himself was beaten, tarred, jailed. There were shootings and fires and calls for vengeance on both sides. Finally, the governor of Missouri himself ordered the Mormons to leave his state or be "exterminated."[1]

Smith and his followers settled in Commerce, Illinois, which he renamed Nauvoo. By 1844, Smith had approximately 35,000 converts. The following year, he was jailed for inciting a riot. A mob of militiamen, who concealed their identities, broke into the jail and killed Smith.

The leadership of the Mormon Church was taken over by Brigham Young, who believed the Mormons should continue the move westward. Having read John Charles Frémont's description of the valley of the Great Salt Lake in Utah, Young determined that it was the place for Mormons to build their church and city.

The journey began in the spring of 1846. Young had organized the Mormon migration in detail. Each caravan was divided into groups that were commanded by a captain and supervised by lieutenants. The movements of each day were strictly scheduled with the rising bugle at 5:00 a.m. and the departure bugle at 7:00 a.m. sharp.

The first caravan of wagons stopped at selected intervals to plant fields with crops that could be harvested by later caravans. In turn, a later group replanted the fields. The caravan of this Mormon migration eventually strung out over 300 miles (483 km) as 16,000 Mormons made it to winter

The Migration of a Culture

The Mormons experienced the same drudgery and hard work of migrating westward as other emigrants. But unlike individual families who chose to move West, the choice was not entirely their own. The Mormon leaders felt the church needed a permanent and more isolated place for its members to practice their religion without persecution. Their trip to the West was the migration of a people, religion, and culture.

Members of the Church of Jesus Christ of Latter-Day Saints were prepared to make sacrifices, like biblical saints, for their new religion. They formed a tightly knit church community and tried to stand against those who wanted to destroy them and their church.

Until 1890, the Mormons practiced polygamy, which allowed one Mormon man to have more than one wife. Because the early Mormon Church had more women than men, some historians believe this may have been the reason the men could have several wives. However, people of other religions thought polygamy was immoral, which was part of the reason for persecuting Mormons. The Mormons also were eager to convert people to their religion, which angered others. Because the Mormons were persecuted in Ohio, Missouri, and Illinois, they created their own city in what would become Utah.

This sculpture depicts how the Mormon emigrants of the 1850s crossed the Western Plains with handcarts.

quarters in Omaha, Nebraska. By the summer of 1847, the Mormons reached the Salt Lake valley, which marked the end of a 1,300-mile (2,092-km) journey. The Mormons soon started building their new home in what would become Salt Lake City.

Gold!

The discovery of gold in California also drastically increased traffic on the Oregon Trail. On January 24, 1848, carpenter James Marshall was building a mill for John Sutter in California. In the process, he found large flakes of what looked like gold. After testing these, Marshall and Sutter determined the flakes were indeed gold. The news of their discovery soon spread. Suddenly, travel to California increased as many sought to make a fortune in gold.

While there were several routes to get to California, the only one that did not involve a sea voyage was overland travel. Most gold seekers, nicknamed forty-niners because so many headed for California in 1849, took the land route. They followed the Oregon Trail until it forked in Idaho and then headed southwest for California. Of those who headed to the West in hopes of finding gold, approximately 90 percent were men. Traffic on the trail increased from an estimated 4,000 in 1848 to 30,000 in 1849 and to a high of 55,000 in 1850.

Janette Riker

When tragedy struck, one young woman learned how to fend for herself at a time when many thought a woman alone would not survive. In September 1849, Janette Riker was on her way to Oregon with her father and two brothers. While they were in Montana, the three men went off to hunt, but they never returned. Left completely alone, Janette knew she could not continue across the mountains by herself. She constructed a hut and used the stove, blankets, and provisions from the wagon as well as a load of firewood. Because she had no meat, she slaughtered one of her oxen and salted the meet to preserve it for winter. Having survived the winter, she was found by Native Americans in the spring. Amazed that she had survived on her own, they took her west to her original destination.

CALIFORNIA GOLD RUSH 1849

USA
33

1999

This US postage stamp depicts miners prospecting in the foothills of the Sierra Nevada Mountains during the 1849 Gold Rush.

The emigrants who traveled west seeking gold may have started their journeys in covered wagons, hoping for a fresh start and a new home. But soon, the forty-niners were frantic to reach the gold fields of California as quickly as possible. The journey was often treated as a race—the winner would become rich and the loser would find nothing.

On his way to California in 1849, James Evans described the scene:

The whole emigration is wild and frantic with a desire to be pressing forward . . . . Whenever a wagon unluckily gets stuck in the mud in crossing some little rut, the other trains behind make a universal rush to try to pass that wagon and get ahead of each other. Amid the yelling, popping of whips and cursing, perhaps a wagon wheel is broken, two or three men knocked down in a fight, and twenty guns drawn out of the wagons. All of this occasioned by a delay of perhaps two minutes and a half. [2]

Despite their hopes, few miners were successful. Those who arrived first mined the gold that was easily accessible on their claim. That left others to work for the mining companies that profited the most.

A Changing Trail

One of the men who had joined the Great Migration of 1843 was Missouri farmer Jesse Applegate. He joined his two brothers and their families on a wagon train led by Marcus Whitman. After leaving

A Day with the Cow Column

Jesse Applegate, as the leader of the Cow Column, is one of the best-known emigrants to travel the Oregon Trail. He wrote one of the best narratives of what daily life was like on the trail.

His book's title, *A Day with the Cow Column*, refers to the wagon train that Applegate traveled with in 1843. Because the emigrants who were not traveling with cattle refused to guard other families' cattle at night, the wagon train split into two groups. The Cow Column separated from the main group. While they used the same guides, they traveled separately but had to keep up with the main group while herding several thousand cattle.

their guide and their wagons at Fort Walla Walla, Jesse and his brother constructed boats to travel the Columbia River to Fort Vancouver. Jesse and one of his brothers lost sons who drowned during the river journey.

In 1846, Jesse created a new, safer trail from Nevada along the California Trail and up to Oregon. This trail avoided the dangerous river journey and brought emigrants to Oregon's Willamette Valley by a safer land route.

In 1853, another 3,500 emigrants used this new route to reach Oregon. Instead of being one well-traveled trail, the Oregon Trail was now part of a network of trails, and eventually roads, leading west.

Those who traveled west on the Oregon Trail in the 1860s had a much different experience than that of the first emigrants. Many rivers that had been difficult or treacherous

Becoming a State

In 1846, the Oregon Treaty between the United States and Great Britain divided the territory of Oregon. Great Britain received what is now British Columbia, and Canada. The United States received what is now Washington, Idaho, and Oregon. Oregon Territory, as it was called, became the state of Oregon in 1859.

to cross now had bridges and ferries. Government officials had used dynamite to flatten some of the most difficult hills and to widen narrow areas of the trail. In addition, there were now many more choices for a route west. New side trails and cutoffs had been created because they were easier or because emigrants were forging new routes to gold-mining areas such as Nevada and Colorado. Some cities had stagecoach stations and more amenities for travelers. By 1861, telegraph lines were strung along the entire route.

The Oregon Land Law

Another enticement for those who considered moving westward was the Oregon Donation Land Act, which was signed into law by President Millard Fillmore in 1850. The law, commonly called the Oregon Land Law, allowed emigrants to Oregon to choose claims of land that would become their property simply by living on it for four years:

> Granted to every white settler or occupant of the public lands . . . above the age of eighteen years, being a citizen of the United States, or having made a declaration according to law, of his intention to become a citizen . . . and who

shall have resided upon and cultivated the same for four consecutive years.[3]

When the act expired on December 1, 1855, more than 2.5 million acres (1,011,714 ha) of land were given away in 7,437 claims. The guarantee of free land to any emigrant who settled on and cultivated his claim for four years pulled more people to the area.

During the Civil War, emigration on the Oregon Trail decreased, but it increased when the war was over. But as the 1860s came to a close, the end of the trail was already in sight.

*President Millard Fillmore signed the 1850
Oregon Donation Land Act into law.*

An 1846 painting of Oregon City

The End of the Trail

he difficulties of the trail ended when the
emigrants reached Oregon, but it was not
always the wonderful life they had envisioned—at
least not at first. Many spent months camping in
their wagons or in makeshift tents or huts. Those

who arrived in the fall needed to find land and build some sort of shelter immediately in preparation of the coming winter.

Amelia Hadley wrote of her family's arrival in 1851:

> *We may now call ourselves through, they say, and [here] we are in Oregon making our camp in an ugly bottom and no home except our wagons and tent. It is drizzling, and the weather looks dark and gloomy. This is the end of a long and tedious journey.*[1]

Oregon winters were warmer than what many emigrants were accustomed to, but it often rained. Marilla R. Washburn, who arrived in Oregon with her family in 1852, recalled her first winter, "My most vivid recollection of that first winter in Oregon is of the weeping skies and of mother and I also weeping."[2]

Fortunately, many emigrants had family and friends living in Oregon

"The seven girls slept in the loft and the younger ones slept on the floor in the front room by the fireplace. Father in exchange for our housing taught school to the tenant children and at night made furniture consisting of chairs, tables, brooms and bedsteads."[3]

—Inez Parker, describing her new life in Oregon in 1849

who could take them in or help them get established. Because money was scarce, many emigrants bartered to get what they needed. The friendships and spirit of togetherness that developed on the Oregon Trail continued once the emigrants reached their new home. They often helped each other out.

THE PONY EXPRESS

Those who made the journey to the West from the settled East often became homesick for news from family and friends. Before telegraph lines reached the West, communications were made by mail and carried by railroads or by private mail services such as the Pony Express.

The Pony Express was a system of stations set up 10 to 15 miles (16–24 km) apart on the route from Saint Joseph, Missouri, to Sacramento, California. Riders raced from station to station, changing to a fresh horse at each station. At every eighth station, riders handed over their mailbags to fresh riders.

The route crossed the Rocky Mountains and South Pass at an elevation of approximately 8,000 feet (2,438 m). Riders rode through blizzards, rain, and the fear of a Native American attack.

A letter could reach California in just under ten days. However, the Pony Express lasted only 18 months, from April 1860 to October 1861. Telegraph wires had been completed all along the route, and the Pony Express riders—including the famous Buffalo Bill Cody—were no longer needed.

An Ending and a New Beginning

By the 1860s, the Oregon Trail was a well-worn and clearly defined roadway to the West. The wheels had left deep grooves in many places. Where they had become too deep, new roads had been worn in beside the old. All along the trail, possessions such as furniture and heirlooms had been discarded when the tired animals could

Traveling the Oregon Trail Again and Again

In 1852, Ezra Meeker took his family along the Oregon Trail and settled in Washington Territory. But Meeker was different than other Oregon Trail travelers. He made the trip again in 1906 at the age of 75, using oxen and a wagon just as he did during his first trip. He often stopped to give speeches that emphasized the importance of keeping history—such as the story of emigrants on the trail—alive. Although the trip was difficult, and Meeker's oxen died, he made the trip in great shape.

Meeker made the trip again in 1910. In 1915, he made the trip by automobile. In 1924, at the age of 93, he traveled the Oregon Trail again, but this time he traveled by air. Meeker was making plans for yet another trip with the support of car manufacturer Henry Ford. However, Meeker died in December of 1928, at the age of 98, before he could make this final trip.

Building the Transcontinental Railroad in the late 1860s

no longer haul the extra weight. Worn-out animals had been abandoned beside the trail to fend for themselves. Carcasses of animals and graves of those who died along the way were a frequent sight.

On May 10, 1869, at Promontory Point, in what would eventually become the state of Utah, a symbolic golden spike was hammered into place to celebrate the completion of the transcontinental railroad. The last rail had been laid to join the

Union Pacific and the Central Pacific Railroads. With 2,000 miles (3,219 km) of rails, the Missouri River was now linked with the Pacific coast. What once took four to six months by wagon could now be traveled in six days by train.

This was the beginning of the end of the Oregon Trail. Yet, traveling by rail with all of one's possessions was expensive, and many emigrants could not afford it. In addition, emigrants needed their livestock and wagons to set up a new home in Oregon. The overland trail remained the least expensive mode of transportation.

However, much of the land had been claimed by Native Americans. In many places, the best land had already been claimed. The crowding and lack of opportunity that originally drove the emigrants out of the East slowly started to affect the West as well.

The golden age of migration on the Oregon Trail was over. In 1890, Robert D. Porter, superintendent of the 1890 US census, announced that the frontier no longer existed:

Up to and including 1880 the country had a frontier of settlement, but at present the unsettled area has been broken into by isolated bodies of settlement that there can hardly be said to be a frontier line. In the discussion of its extent, its westward movement, etc., it cannot, therefore, any longer have a place in the census reports.[4]

The last wagons that rolled across the Oregon Trail occurred in the 1880s. Some were travelers whose families could not afford train tickets. A few passed through as late as the early 1900s. Most of these trips were made out of nostalgia. This was the case for Ezra Meeker, who traveled the route in 1906 as a way to keep the history of the trail alive.

The Legacy of the Oregon Trail

Generations after the last wagon trains traveled the trail, the ruts left by the thousands of wagons between Missouri and Oregon are still visible. Towns and cities have built up along the original trail route. Much of it is covered by modern highways that follow the same path. Still, these

Francis Parkman

Francis Parkman was born in Boston, Massachusetts, in 1823. He became one of the most famous chroniclers of the Oregon Trail experience. *The Oregon Trail: Sketches of Prairie and Rocky-Mountain Life* was first written as a series of 21 installments in the *Knickerbocker* magazine from 1847 to 1849. In 1849, it was published as a book. Though the book covers only the first section of the trail, it includes a description of a three-week hunting trip that Parkman participated in with a tribe of Ogala Sioux. Parkman's descriptions of the trail and those traveling on it are some of the most vivid personal narratives of the Oregon migration.

*A wagon without its canvas cover at the Oregon Trail
Interpretive Center in Baker City, Oregon*

wagon train ruts remain and remind Americans of
the sacrifices and hardships required of those who
left behind everything they knew and struck out for a
new place with new opportunities.

As author Lillian Schlissel wrote in *Women's Diaries
of the Westward Journey*:

> *The qualities of mind and heart that led men and women to
> choose to make the . . . journey are difficult to recapture. An
> intense hunger for land and for gold and a heady confidence
> in their own strength combined to catapult the emigrants*

A National Historic Trail

In 1978, the US Park Service named the 2,170-mile (3,492-km) Oregon Trail as a National Historic Trail. Although much of the trail is now on privately owned land, the US Park Service maintains 125 landmarks and more than 300 miles (483 km) of trail that have changed very little since the emigrants traveled it. Landmarks such as Chimney Rock, Independence Rock, and Scott's Bluff are open for visitors.

across a continent. They refused to be discouraged. With a boundless, even foolhardy courage, they suppressed the drama of their personal lives for the larger drama that lay before them.[5]

The trip was not easy, and thousands died along the way and never reached their goal of a fresh start in a new place. But for those who did arrive in Oregon, the memory of their journey would stay with them as a proud accomplishment and an important contribution to the development of the United States.

Ruts were worn into the rock by wagon trains on the Oregon Trail.

TIMELINE

1542	1803	1805
The first European explorers from Spain see the Oregon coast.	The area of the United States nearly doubles with the Louisiana Purchase.	Meriwether Lewis and William Clark's expedition reaches the Oregon coast.

1832	1836	1837
Captain Benjamin Bonneville's expedition is the first to cross the Rocky Mountains with wagons.	The Whitman party proves the trail to Oregon was passable by wagon train.	The Panic of 1837 convinces many people to set out for Oregon.

1807	1811	1812
Manuel Lisa constructs Fort Raymond along the Yellowstone River.	John Jacob Astor sets up the Astoria fur trading post in Oregon.	Robert Stuart discovers the South Pass through the Rocky Mountains.

1842	1842–1844	1843
The first wagon train travels to Oregon.	John Charles Frémont makes accurate maps of much of the West.	The Great Migration begins as the first large wagon train leaves for Oregon.

TIMELINE

1845	1846	1846
The Emigrants' Guide to Oregon and California by Lansford Warren Hastings is published.	The United States and Great Britain formally divide Oregon Country.	The Mormon migration begins as the Mormons travel westward to the Great Salt Lake.

1859	1869	1890
Oregon becomes a state.	The transcontinental railroad is completed at Promontory Point, Utah.	The US census reports that there is no longer a western frontier.

1847

1848

1850

Narcissa and Marcus Whitman are killed during a Native American attack on their mission.

Gold is discovered at Sutter's Mill in California.

The Oregon Donation Land Law makes free land available to emigrants who live on the land for four years.

1906

1978

Ezra Meeker begins making trips along the old Oregon Trail route to preserve its history.

The US Congress creates the Oregon National Historic Trail.

ESSENTIAL FACTS

DATE OF EVENT

1841 through the 1880s

PLACE OF EVENT

The trail of approximately 2,170 miles (3,492 km) began from various jumping-off points, such as the cities of Independence and Saint Joseph in Missouri, to what is now the state of Oregon.

KEY PLAYERS

- ❖ Thomas Jefferson
- ❖ Meriwether Lewis
- ❖ William Clark
- ❖ Robert Stuart
- ❖ John Charles Frémont

HIGHLIGHTS OF EVENT

- ❖ The Louisiana Purchase in 1803 doubled the size of the United States. This gave explorers and traders access to the Mississippi River trade route and the area between the known United States and the Rocky Mountains.
- ❖ In 1812, Astorian Robert Stuart set out eastward from Oregon traveling south of Lewis and Clark's expedition route. Stuart discovered a pass through the Rocky Mountains that became known as the South Pass. Unlike the other passes through the Rocky Mountains, this was a gentle slope rather than a steep, mountainous drop-off. Decades later, it was used as part of the Oregon Trail because it was the only place where wagons could easily travel across the mountain range.

❖ In 1836, the Whitman group of missionaries was the first to travel to Oregon by covered wagons.

❖ In 1843, thousands of emigrants made the four- to five-month trip to Oregon in covered wagon trains, carrying approximately 1,600 to 2,500 pounds (726 to 1,134 kg) in food, belongings, and tools.

❖ From 1843 to 1869, approximately 350,000 to 500,000 emigrants followed the trail to Oregon. Approximately 20,000 to 30,000 of these emigrants died while on the trail.

❖ In 1869, the advent of the transcontinental railroad ended the Great Migration on the Oregon Trail. Many, however, still traveled by wagon train in order to bring their belongings.

Quote

"The qualities of mind and heart that led men and women to choose to make the . . . journey are difficult to recapture. An intense hunger for land and for gold and a heady confidence in their own strength combined to catapult the emigrants across a continent. They refused to be discouraged. With a boundless, even foolhardy courage, they suppressed the drama of their personal lives for the larger drama that lay before them."—*Lillian Schlissel, Women's Diaries of the Westward Journey*

GLOSSARY

boomtown
A town that has grown quickly as the result of sudden prosperity.

census
An official counting of a population.

claim
A piece of land that has been claimed, especially public land that has been requested for private use.

congestion
Overcrowded, clogged conditions.

emigrant
A person who moves to settle elsewhere in his or her native country or another country.

epidemic
A disease that affects many people at the same time and spreads from person to person.

expanse
A large uninterrupted space or area.

expedition
A journey or voyage made for a specific purpose.

financier
A person skilled in running large financial operations or providing money for them.

formalized
To make an official or authorized acceptance of a contract or agreement.

formation
A body of rocks in a geological shape or pattern.

geyser
A spring that intermittently sends jets of hot water or steam into the air.

heirloom
> A family possession handed down from generation to generation.

incapacitate
> To deprive of ability or strength, to disable.

itinerant preacher
> One who travels a circuit from town to town to preach the gospel.

manifest destiny
> The doctrine that it was the destiny of the United States to expand across the entire North American continent.

massacre
> The unnecessary killing of a large number of people or animals.

migration
> A group of people moving from one country, region, or place to another.

missionary
> A person sent by a church into an area to educate, help, and convert other people to the missionary's religion.

pelt
> The untanned hide or skin of an animal.

pirogue
> A boat similar to a canoe in shape and size.

revelation
> Something revealed, explained, or communicated.

specimen
> A sample plant, animal, mineral, or part from a specific area.

ADDITIONAL RESOURCES

SELECTED BIBLIOGRAPHY

Carnes, Mark C., ed. *MacMillan Compendium of American History*. New York: Simon, 1996. Print.

Faragher, John Mack. *Women and Men on the Overland Trail*. New Haven, CT: Yale UP, 1979. Print.

Schlissel, Lillian. *Women's Diaries of the Westward Journey*. New York: Schocken, 1982. Print.

Ward, Geoffrey C. *The West: An Illustrated History*. Boston: Little, 1996. Print.

Wexler, Alan. *Atlas of Westward Expansion*. New York: Facts on File, 1995. Print.

FURTHER READINGS

McNees, Tim. *The Oregon Trail: Pathway to the West*. New York: Chelsea, 2009. Milestones in American History. Print.

Meeker, Ezra. *Personal Experiences on the Oregon Trail Sixty Years Ago*. N.p., n.d. Print.

Web Links

To learn more about the Oregon Trail, visit ABDO Publishing Company online at **www.abdopublishing.com**. Web sites about the Oregon Trail are featured on our Book Links page. These links are routinely monitored and updated to provide the most current information available.

Places to Visit

National Frontier Trails Museum
318 West Pacific, Independence, MO 64050
816-325-7575
www.ci.independence.mo.us/nftm/Default.aspx
Independence, Missouri, was one of the jumping-off points for the Oregon Trail. This museum, interpretive center, and research library focus on the history of the principle western trails in the United States.

National Historic Oregon Trail Interpretive Center
22267 Oregon Highway 86, Baker City, OR 97814-0987
541-523-1843
www.blm.gov/or/oregontrail/
The interpretive center presents living history demonstrations, interpretive programs, exhibits, presentations, and interpretive trails.

National Oregon/California Trail Center
320 North Fourth Street, Montpelier, ID 83254
208-847-3800
www.oregontrailcenter.org/
Visit the interpretive center and experience a simulated trek along the Oregon Trail.

SOURCE NOTES

Chapter 1. The Long Trail West

1. Catherine Sager Pringle. "Across the Plains in 1844."
New Perspectives on the West. Film Project and WETA, 2001. Web.
7 Jan. 2011.

2. Geoffrey C. Ward. *The West: An Illustrated History*. Boston: Little,
1996. Print. 92.

3. Joy Hakim. *A History of Us: Liberty for All? 1800–1860*. 2nd ed.
New York: Oxford UP, 1994. Print. 34.

4. Lillian Schlissel. *Women's Diaries of the Westward Journey*. New
York: Schocken, 1982. Print. 43.

5. Ibid. 216.

6. Geoffrey C. Ward. *The West: An Illustrated History*. Boston: Little,
1996. Print. 95.

Chapter 2. An Expanding Country

1. "Louisiana Purchase Treaty, 1803." *Archives.gov*. National
Archives and Records Administration, n.d. Web. 7 Nov. 2010.

2. Geoffrey C. Ward. *The West: An Illustrated History*. Boston: Little,
1996. Print. 39.

3. "Thomas Jefferson on Politics and Government." *Thomas
Jefferson*. University of Virginia Library, n.d. Web. 12 Jan. 2011.

4. Geoffrey C. Ward. *The West: An Illustrated History*. Boston: Little,
1996. Print. 47.

5. Ibid.

Chapter 3. The Trailblazers

1. Geoffrey C. Ward. *The West: An Illustrated History*. Boston: Little,
1996. Print. 56–57.

2. Ibid. 57–58.

Chapter 4. Manifest Destiny

1. Nancy Wilson Ross. *Westward the Women*. San Francisco: North Point, 1985. Print. 7.

2. John D. Unruh. *The Plains Across*. U of Illinois P, 1993. Web. 7 Jan. 2011.

3. Lillian Schlissel. *Women's Diaries of the Westward Journey*. New York: Schocken, 1982. Print. 20–21.

4. John L. O'Sullivan. "Annexation." *The United States Magazine and Democratic Review,* July 1845. Historytools.org, 18 July 2004. Web. 14 Nov. 2010.

5. Lansford W. Hastings. "CHAPTER XV. THE EQUIPMENT, SUPPLIES, AND THE METHOD OF TRAVELING." *The Emigrants' Guide to Oregon and California*. 1845. U of Virginia, 6 May 1998. Web. 12 Jan. 2011.

Chapter 5. On the Trail

1. Francis Parkman, *The Oregon Trail: Sketches of Prairie and Rocky Mountain Life*. Boston: Little, 1920. Web. 7 Jan. 2011.

2. John Hawkins Clark. Compiled by Jim Tompkins. "Mileposts Along the Oregon Trail." N.p., n.d. Web. 7 Jan. 2011.

3. "Oregon Trail Mileposts." Oregon-California Trails Association, 2011. Web. 7 Jan. 2011.

4. Sanford Wexler. *Westward Expansion: An Eyewitness History*. New York: Facts on File, 1991. Print. 155.

5. Lillian Schlissel. *Women's Diaries of the Westward Journey*. New York: Schocken, 1982. Print. 195.

Chapter 6. Life in a Wagon Train

1. Mike Trinklein and Steve Boettcher. "Power." *The Oregon Trail*. N.p., n.d. Web. 19 Nov. 2010.

2. Mike Trinklein and Steve Boettcher. "The Diary of Mrs. Amelia Stewart Knight (1853)." *The Oregon Trail*, N.p., n.d. Web. 21 Jan. 2011.

3. Nancy Wilson Ross. *Westward the Women*. San Francisco: North Point. 1985. Print. 10.

SOURCE NOTES CONTINUED

Chapter 7. Dangers on the Trail

1. Catherine Sager Pringle. "Across the Plains in 1844." *New Perspectives on the West*. West Film Project and WETA, 2001. Web. 7 Jan. 2011.

2. Lillian Schlissel. *Women's Diaries of the Westward Journey*. New York: Schocken, 1982. Print. 13.

3. Mike Trinklein and Steve Boettcher. "Hardships on the Oregon Trail." N.p., n.d. Web. 19 Nov. 2010.

4. Ibid.

5. Francis Parkman. *The Oregon Trail: Sketches of Prairie and Rocky Mountain Life*. Boston: Little, 1920. Web. 16 Jan. 2010.

6. Lillian Schlissel. *Women's Diaries of the Westward Journey*. New York: Schocken, 1982. Print. 55.

7. Ibid. 209.

Chapter 8. A Home in the West

1. Geoffrey C. Ward. *The West: An Illustrated History*. Boston: Little, 1996. Print. 101.

2. Ibid. 126.

3. "Document: The Donation Land Claim Act, 1850." *CCRH. org*. Center for Columbia River History, n.d. Web. 13 Jan. 2011.

Chapter 9. The End of the Trail

1. "Triumph and Tragedy: Women's Voices from the Oregon Trail." *OBP.org*. Oregon Public Broadcasting, 1999. Web. 7 Jan. 2011.

2. Ibid.

3. Ibid.

4. Calvin DeArmond Davis. "The Frederick Jackson Turner Census: Its Indiana Memorial." N.p., n.d. Web. 21 Nov. 2010.

5. Lillian Schlissel. *Women's Diaries of the Westward Journey*. New York: Schocken, 1982. Print. 72.

INDEX

Index Continued

ABOUT THE AUTHOR

Marcia Amidon Lusted is the author of more than 40 books for young readers and has written many magazine articles. She is an assistant editor for six magazines, a writing instructor, and a musician. She lives in New Hampshire with her family.

PHOTO CREDITS

North Wind/North Wind Picture Archives, cover, 3, 45, 95, 99 (bottom); After Eugene Antoine Samuel Lavieille/Getty Images, 6; Getty Images, 11, 90, 98; Geoffrey Clifford/Getty Images, 13; AP Images, 14, 18, 23, 24, 26, 31, 35, 39, 46, 50, 53, 56, 60, 63, 64, 69, 73, 78, 80, 85, 93, 96, 97, 99 (top); FPG/Getty Images, 36; Bob Pardue—Midwest/Alamy, 55; Red Line Editorial, Inc., 74; Picture History, 86